Indian Festive Flavours

Indian Festive Flavours
South Indian Vegetarian Specialties

by
Priya

iUniverse, Inc.
New York   Bloomington

iUniverse books may be ordered through booksellers or by contacting:

iUniverse
1663 Liberty Drive
Bloomington, IN 47403
www.iuniverse.com
1-800-Authors (1-800-288-4677)

ISBN: 978-1-4401-2997-1 (sc)
ISBN: 978-1-4401-2998-8 (ebook)

Printed in the United States of America

iUniverse rev. date: 04/02/2009

To Amma – the most fantastic cook I know!

To Appa & to Steve, my husband, both of whom have supported this endeavour and my cooking, whole heartedly

And a special thanks

To Kate and Andy – who came up with the title suggestions

CONTENTS

preface

Food has always played a very important role in our family life and all our breakfasts, lunches, dinners and "tiffins" were a ritual that we engaged in with utmost concentration. As a child, I remember my mother saying, "If you don't enjoy your meal, it is not going to add any value to your body". I was never forced to eat what I did not like. Instead, I was encouraged to eat my favourite food and my mother always took the pain of cooking it exactly the way I appreciated it (spoilt brat, moi!!)

Interestingly enough, this attitude meant that I grew up loving my food, eating all the greens on my plate. Unlike many of my friends in school, I never disliked any vegetable. I believe, even until today, that everything can be made to taste delicious if cooked properly. As a child, I remember all my meals coming up fresh from the kitchen - piping hot. Now that I have grown up and read a lot about yoga and health, I realise that enjoying your meal is indeed the way to a true yogic diet.

My mother came from Tamil Nadu and my father, from Kerala - both states in the South of India. Our food at home was a mix of Tamilian and Malayali vegetarian cuisine - both equally delightful. Rice was a staple diet and she could turn the most inane vegetables into a work of art.

Festivals were celebrated religiously and each festival had its trademark dishes and rituals. Living in Delhi, my mother feared that I may never learn about the South and therefore went out of her way to celebrate every festival. I was a curious child and would try to find out more about why they were celebrated - but somehow, I always felt that she could tell me more about how they were celebrated and I usually picked up the religious significance of most of them from my books.

I never cooked anything until I was in college. I remember having a disastrous stint with "Rasam", a South Indian soup, once when my mum was away tending to my grandmother in the hospital and I gave up the ambition to become a good cook. Living in Delhi with many friends from Punjab and UP, I loved the food from the north and slowly started learning how to cook. Genetics play a big role and I found that cooking could be the most relaxing of pastimes.

I started making my favourite dishes from my childhood once I discovered that I could cook reasonably well. I would call my mother on the phone and ask her for the recipe and follow her instructions to the T. It is when I started writing down some of her recipes that I thought of putting this book together. I wanted this to reflect my happy culinary memories of childhood and my mother's amazing skills with the ladle.

My mother, beyond all my doubts, is indeed the best cook in the world to me.

This book is dedicated to her and to my grandmother who enjoys my mum's cooking almost as much as I do. This is also dedicated to my father who contributed hugely to our meals by laying the table every day - and otherwise stayed thankfully away from the kitchen. And last but not least, a word in praise of my husband, who delights in eating anything that I cook and has provided fantastic moral support while I tried to pen this book!

glossary

Difficulty Levels	⊕ Simple; ⊕⊕ Medium Difficulty; ⊕⊕⊕ Difficult or time consuming
Cooking/Preparation time	These are just an indication - will vary with your speed of work
Channa Dal	Yellow Split Peas. Commonly available in Health food shops, Asian shops and supermarkets
Ghee	Clarified Butter - available in the Asian section of Supermarkets; You can use white unsalted butter as a substitute
Jaggery	Raw Cane Sugar. Available in Asian Shops/Supermarket. You can substitute this with Brown Muscovado/Cane Sugar.
Mung Dal	Yellow split Mung bean. Available in Supermarkets
Urad Dal	White split gram. Available in Asian shops.

Tur/Arhar Dal	A yellow Dal found in Indian shops or Supermarkets. An oily version is also available and can be used in the same way.
Asafoetida	Also called Hing. A spice that's used in very small quantities and has a pungent flavour. It's available in a powdered form in most large Supermarkets, in the spice section
Sesame Oil	Also called Til Oil. This is un-toasted Sesame oil that's available in Organic health food shops. Do not use toasted oil as that significantly affects the taste. You can substitute sesame oil with the same quantity of Sunflower oil.
Coconut Oil	Available in Health food stores and in the Asian section of Supermarkets. It is also popular for beauty and hair care in India. Choose un-perfumed coconut oil for cooking as oil for other purposes often has additives like lemon juice and herbs, which could affect the taste.

Tava	This is a flat Pancake pan or griddle that you can get in Indian shops. Some big home stores also sell Cast-iron or non-stick flat pans that are good substitutes. Ideally a Tava should have a very low or no rim. Use a flat wooden pancake-flip in conjunction with the Tava.
Karai	A Karai (pronounced Kadai) is a deep round frying pan used in Indian cooking. It is available in the home-ware section of many large Supermarkets and also in Asian shops. Similar to a small wok
Mixie	Most of the grinding for Indian cooking is done with a mixer that has an attachment for wet and dry grinding. You would be able to get one in Indian shops or large home stores. Alternately, you may be able to use a coffee grinder or a mortar and pestle - and a bit of elbow grease!

helpful hints and tips

Tarka: The process of warming a tablespoon of oil and adding mustard or cumin seeds is called Tarka. It is very common in Indian cooking. Make sure the oil is hot but not smoking. Add black mustard seeds and wait until you hear them spluttering - at this stage you may see some seeds actually pop out of the pan. Have the rest of the ingredients that need to be added ready at hand so that you don't burn the mustard seeds. Indian cooking uses black mustard seeds and not brown ones.

Chillies: Chillies are commonly used in most recipes. If you are not keen on very spicy food, make sure you remove the seeds before chopping the chillies up. Also, if a recipe demands that you fry the chillies, you must cut them or break them before dropping them in oil as whole chillies can explode.

Tamarind: You can buy fresh tamarind or concentrate in the Asian section of large Supermarkets. The strength of the concentrate varies - so be careful about adding too much from the beginning. If using fresh tamarind to make a paste, use double the quantity of this paste (as the recipe).

Pressure Cooking: For those of you skilled enough to use a pressure cooker, it is a great time saver. It does take a bit of getting used to and I'd recommend that you follow the instructions that come with the cooker meticulously. Normally, one measure of rice takes around two and a half measures of water to cook. A similar ratio will work with Dal as well.

Deep Frying: The oil should be hot but not smoking. One way to test the heat is to try a small portion of whatever you plan to fry first. If the test portion rises to the top immediately, the oil is hot enough. If it turns brown immediately, the oil is too hot and needs to cool down. If the portion does not rise for a while, you need to wait a bit before trying again. Never drop things from a distance into hot oil - if you're nervous, you can use two spoons to gently spoon your paste into the oil. The shapes won't be perfect, but you don't have to worry about splashing yourself. Please never leave frying oil unattended on the hob.

Ideally, frying should be done on a gas hob, as it is very difficult to turn the heat down and manage the temperature otherwise.

Coconut: You can buy fresh coconuts in the exotic fruits and vegetables section of Supermarkets. Some of the larger markets also sell frozen grated coconut. The frozen version is much easier and less messy to deal with. The third alternative is to buy desiccated coconut that is available in plenty in the bakery section of supermarkets. However, this does not taste as good as the other two versions.

If you purchase a fresh coconut, you will need to drain the water inside by piercing holes through the eyes on one end of the fruit. After that the nut can be split open to reveal white flesh inside. Scoop this flesh with a knife and grind this in a food processor. You can freeze this coconut in freezer bags and use as required. Defrost the required amount in a microwave.

Grinding of spices and masalas: Traditionally, there were a variety of stone implements and large stone mortar and pestle used for grinding. However, these are very heavy and take a great deal of skill and time. An alternative is to use a good food processor/Mixer with an attachment for wet/dry grinding. Make sure that all the ingredients that you are going to grind have cooled down before you grind them as otherwise the heat can seal and jam the grinding container. Add very little water while grinding "masala pastes" given in the recipes. If need be, you can always stop and add a bit more. If you start with too much water, the spices will not grind and mix properly. This is particularly important while grinding coconut.

Dry Roasting Spices: Whole spices, such as cloves, peppercorns, cumin etc. are often roasted in a pan without any oil or water in order to enhance their fragrance. Heat a small wok or pan over medium heat and add the required spices. Stir constantly - the spices should start browning slightly. Remove from heat. If you are roasting whole red chillies, remember to cut them into two as they can explode. Whole peppercorns can also explode if heated for too long - keep the heat low and remove the peppercorns after roasting for a minute or two.

Measurements: Indian recipes do not use very precise measurements. Many of the measures are rounded up and as long as you are using the same sized cup or spoon to measure out the ingredients in a recipe, you will do fine.

Cup: The average cup measures around 7 fl.oz or 210 ml. If you are using a larger cup, you may need to increase the quantity of the rest of the ingredients accordingly.

Teaspoon: A Teaspoon is expected to be filled level to the brim. The volume of a teaspoon will be about 1/6 fl.oz or 5 ml.

Tablespoon: This is also expected to be filled level to the brim. One Tablespoon is equal to three Teaspoons or around ½ fl.oz or 15 ml.

Weight: Weight is mentioned in Grams in some recipes. For conversion of grams to millilitres or fluid ounces (fl.oz), please refer to the following conversion scheme.

Weight in grams	Oz (or fl.oz)	Millilitres
25 grams	1 oz	30 ml
75 grams	3 oz	90 ml
400 grams	16 oz	480 ml

festivals in january

The month of January is an important one as we celebrate Bohi, Pongal and Kanu around the middle of the month. These are harvest festivals. During the festival of Pongal, it is considered auspicious to let food spill and overflow while cooking. This signifies the coming of good things in abundance.

I remember going to my grandmother's house to celebrate Kanu. If there was one thing that I hated about all the tamilian festivals - it was getting up very early in the morning. Kanu was particularly bad as we had to go out doors and place a little bit of everything that was cooked on a banana leaf and offer it to the birds at some unearthly hour, in the freezing Delhi winter cold. The idea was to pray for a life of happiness with your clan, just like the flocking birds.

But later on, I would forget about all that, as I would get to eat the food. "Poli" is my favourite sweet dish and that was the highlight of the Pongal, Kanu and Bohi trio of festivals for me.

Bohi

poli (coconut pancakes)

2

Indian Festive Flavours

⊕ ⊕

Serves: 4
Preparation time: 6 hours
Cooking time: 1 hour

Ingredients:

Channa Dal
(dry roasted very slightly): 1 Cup
Sugar: 2 Cups
Powdered Cardamom: ½ Teaspoon
Powdered Coconut: 1 Tablespoon
Plain Flour: 400grams
Food colour (Optional): ½ Teaspoon
Ghee: 1 Teaspoon
Sesame Oil: 3 Tablespoons

Method:

Add the sesame oil and food colour to the flour. Add enough water and knead to make soft dough. Keep this dough in a covered dish overnight or at least for 6 hours.

Pressure-cook the split peas with 2 Cups of water - they need to be very well done. If you are using a pressure cooker, cook them for up to 15 minutes (or 6 -7 whistles). Drain, cool and mash well. Keep aside. If you're not using a pressure cooker, it's advisable to soak them in warm water for a few hours and then boil in a closed pan. When done, they should mash easily.

Meantime, in a pan, add the sugar and just enough water to cover the sugar and bring to boil on low heat. When the sugar dissolves to become thin syrup, add the mashed split peas. Stir the mixture constantly over low heat. Add the ghee. When the mixture is ready, it will leave the sides of the pan and become pulpy. Remove from heat and add the powdered cardamom and coconut. Cool and roll into 15 small balls.

Place a non-stick pan or griddle on the fire over low heat. Sprinkle some flour on the griddle. Take some of the dough and using your hands, flatten it in the shape of a disc. Place the filling inside and pull the sides of the disc to cover the filling completely. Using a little bit of flour, roll this out like a small pancake.

Cook this on the hot griddle until pink spots appear - flip both sides until they are cooked similarly. To serve, add a dollop of ghee and serve hot, after serving the main course.

Bohi

milk poli (saffron-milk pancakes)

Serves: 2-3
Preparation time:
Cooking time: 35 minutes

Ingredients:

Flour: 1 Cup
Milk: ¾ Litre
Powdered Cardamom: ½ Teaspoon
Saffron: ¼ Teaspoon
Powdered Nutmeg: a pinch
Sugar: ½ Cup
Oil: for deep frying

Method:

Using just enough water, knead the flour to make soft dough. Roll the dough into small pancakes (4 inches in diameter).

Dissolve the saffron in a little milk and add to the rest of the milk along with the cardamom, sugar and nutmeg. Heat this over low heat until the consistency of the milk becomes thicker.

In the meantime, over low heat, heat the oil in a frying pan and deep fry all the pancakes and drain over kitchen paper. Drop the pancakes into the milk (one at a time) and press in, using a spoon. Let this soak for 2 minutes. Remove the pancake and place in a serving dish. Repeat with the rest of the pancakes. Pour the leftover milk over the pancakes and serve hot.

Bohi
vadai (dal patties)

🕑
Serves: 3
Preparation time: 3 hours
Cooking time: 30 minutes

Ingredients:

Urad Dal: 1 Cup
Green chillies: 2
Dry red chillies: 1 or 2
Asafoetida: a pinch
Salt: to taste
Oil: for deep frying

Method:

Soak the Split Black Gram for 2-3 hours. Grind the dal with the green and red chillies, asafoetida and salt with a little water to make a smooth, soft but thick paste.

Heat the oil in a Karai or deep frying pan over low heat. To make the vadas, use a thick plastic sheet (like a freezer bag) and wipe it clean with water. Take a tablespoon of the vada mixture on the sheet and flatten slightly, in the shape of a doughnut. Using your finger, make a hole in the centre. Wet your hands to remove this vada and carefully slip it into the frying pan. Deep fry until golden on both sides. Repeat with the rest of the vada mixture. Please look at the Helpful Hints and Tips section for more information on deep-frying.

Serve warm with coconut chutney.

Note:

It is vital to ensure the oil is not too hot - otherwise, the vadas will brown very quickly on the outside but not get cooked fully on the inside.

Bohi
coconut chutney

5

Serves: 3
Preparation time:
Cooking time: 15 minutes

Ingredients:

Grated Coconut: 1 Cup
Green Chillies: 2
Urad Dal: 1 ½ Tablespoons
Curry Leaves: 2-3 leaves
Mustard Seeds: 1 Teaspoon
Sesame Oil: 2 Tablespoons
Salt: to taste

Method:

Set aside 1 Teaspoon of Urad Dal. Heat 1 Tablespoon of oil in a pan and fry the rest of the Urad Dal and chopped green chillies until the chillies turn white and the Dal is light brown. Drain and cool. Grind this mixture with the grated coconut and a little water (1/2 Cup) and salt and decant into a serving bowl.

Heat the rest of the oil and add the mustard seeds. When they splutter, add the reserved Urad Dal and curry leaves. As the dal turns pink, remove from heat and pour on top of the chutney.

You can garnish the chutney with fresh coriander leaves if you are unable to find curry leaves.

The chutney tastes great as a dip and can be stored in the fridge for a day or two.

Pongal

pongal (rice and jaggery pudding)

Indian Festive Flavours

Pongal is traditionally eaten along with sugarcane, aamai vadai, rice and avial.

Serves: 2-3
Preparation time:
Cooking time: 50 minutes

Ingredients:

Mung or Channa dal: 1 Teaspoon
Rice: ¾ Cup
Water: 2 Cups
Powdered jaggery: 1 Cup
Ghee: 5 Teaspoons
Powdered Cardamom: ¼ Teaspoon
Cashew nuts: 1 Tablespoon
Raisins: ½ Tablespoon
Powdered Nutmeg: a pinch

Method:

Boil and cook the dal until soft (should take around 15-20 minutes). Add to the rice and cook with the 2 Cups of water, adding more water if required. The rice should be very well cooked and almost mashed. This would take another 20-30 minutes. Traditionally, the farmers would let the rice overflow from the pot, thus calling it pongal.

Stir in the Jaggery and 3 Teaspoon of ghee - keep the rice over low heat and stir frequently. When the mixture is cooked and comes off from the sides of the pan, remove from heat and add the cardamom. In the remaining ghee, fry the cashew nuts and raisins and add to the pongal along with the nutmeg. Garnish with grated coconut and serve piping hot. This also tastes great when cold, provided the rice has been cooked really well.

Warm Pongal tastes wonderful with a dollop of fresh cream.

Pongal

aamai vadai (savoury dal patties)

Serves: 3-4
Preparation time: 3 hours
Cooking time: 20 minutes

Ingredients:

Urad Dal: 1 Cup
Tur/Arhar dal: 1 Cup
Channa dal: ½ Cup
Green chillies: 2
Dry Red chillies: 2-3
Asafoetida: a pinch
Salt: to taste
Oil: for deep frying

Method:

Soak the dals for 3 hours and grind coarsely with very little water to make a thick paste.

On a thick wet plastic sheet, flatten small balls of the vada batter and deep fry in hot oil until golden brown on both sides. Please look at the Helpful Hints and Tips section for more information on deep-frying.

Serve with Chutney or ketchup.

avial
(mixed vegetables in coconut gravy)

Avial is my favourite curry dish. It's a stew made with seasonal vegetables and coconut and is delicious served with steamed rice. My mother used to explain the goodness in the various vegetables added in avial and this used to make me feel great that I was eating something that was very good for my health but at the same time, simply delicious.

Serves: 3
Preparation time: 5-10 minutes
Cooking time: 25-30 minutes

Ingredients:

White gourd: 100 grams
Pumpkin: 50 grams
Peas: 2 Tablespoons
Beans: 7-8
Potato: 1
Raw banana (optional): ½
Arbi* (boiled and skinned - optional): 3
Yam (boiled and skinned): 1 Cup
Carrot: ½
Tamarind concentrate: ½ Teaspoon
Turmeric powder: ½ Teaspoon
Salt: to taste
Fresh grated coconut: ½ Cup
Cumin seeds: ½ Teaspoon
Green chillies: 2
Yogurt: 1 Tablespoon
Coconut oil: 1 Tablespoon
Curry leaves1 sprig or 7-8 leaves

*   Colacasia or Eddoes – they are a root vegetable available in the exotic vegetables section of large supermarkets

Method:

Skin the gourds, potato, and banana and string the beans. Cut all the vegetables (except peas) to 1-½ inches long strips (1/2 cm wide).

In a pan, add just enough water to cover the vegetables and cook them with salt and turmeric powder. Once cooked, add the Tamarind concentrate and boil well.

In a Mixie, grind the green chillies, grated coconut and cumin seeds with 2 Tablespoon of water. Add this well ground paste to the vegetables. Whisk the yogurt well and add to the vegetables, along with the coconut oil. Garnish with curry leaves and serve hot with boiled rice.

Note:

You can use desiccated coconut if fresh coconut is not available - however reduce the quantity by half and soak it in warm water before grinding.

Kanu
coconut rice

9

Kanu is the 3rd day of the pongal celebrations. A variety of rice dishes would be prepared on this day: Tamarind rice, lemon rice, coconut rice, Sweet candied pongal and curd rice.

Serves: 3-4
Preparation time: 30 minutes
Cooking time: 30 minutes (includes 20 minutes for cooking rice)

Ingredients:

Fresh grated coconut: ½ Cup
Split Black Gram (Urad Dal): 1 ½ Teaspoons
Sesame oil: 5 Teaspoons
Mustard seeds: ¾ Teaspoon
Green chilli: 1
Salt: to taste
Cashew nuts: 1 Tablespoon
Asafoetida: a pinch
Curry leaves: 4-5 leaves
Ghee: 1 Tablespoon
Cooked rice: 1 ½ Cups

Method:

Soak the Split Black Gram (Urad Dal) for half an hour in hot water. In a frying pan, heat the sesame oil and add the mustard seeds. When the seeds splutter, add the chopped green chilli and the drained Split Black Gram. When the dal turns pink, add the coconut and fry over low heat for 2-3 minutes. Add the asafoetida, curry leaves, salt and the cooked rice. Mix well. Heat the ghee and fry the cashew nuts until golden and garnish the rice with this.

Coconut rice can be eaten warm or cold and tastes just as delicious. It tastes great with Okra Raita and Puli Ingi.

puli ingi (ginger and tamarind chutney)

Serves: 3-4
Preparation time:
Cooking time: 20 minutes

Ingredients:

Tamarind concentrate: 1 Tablespoon
Green Chilli: 2
Ginger (chopped fine): 2 Tablespoons
Sesame Seeds (white): 1 Tablespoon
Mustard seeds: 1 Teaspoon
Urad Dal: 1 Teaspoon
Channa Dal: 1 Teaspoon
Sesame Oil: 1 Tablespoon
Turmeric powder: ½ Teaspoon
Salt: to taste
Powdered Jaggery: ¾ Teaspoon

Method:

Heat the oil in a pan and add the Mustard seeds. When they splutter, add the urad dal and channa dal. Fry for a few seconds while the dals turn brown. Finely chop and deseed the green chillies and add this along with ginger to the oil. Fry for a minute. Add turmeric powder and salt. Add half a Cup of water and dissolve the Tamarind concentrate. Add the jaggery and bring to a boil. Reduce the heat and let the chutney bubble away for 5-10 minutes. The water should reduce down and bring the chutney to a paste like consistency. In the meantime, dry roast the sesame seeds until they turn slightly pink. Cool and powder. Add this powder to the chutney and remove from heat.

Serve with coconut rice.

tamarind rice

Serves: 3-4
Preparation time:
Cooking time: 50 minutes (includes 20 minutes for cooking rice)

Ingredients:

Tamarind concentrate: 1 Tablespoon
Sesame oil: 3 Tablespoon
Mustard seeds: ¾ Teaspoon
Channa dal: 1 ½ Teaspoons
Asafoetida: a pinch
Dry red chillies: 6
Raw shelled peanuts: 25 grams
Turmeric powder: ½ Teaspoon
Cooked rice: 2 Cups
Salt: to taste
Sesame oil for garnish: 1 Teaspoon
Curry leaves: 8-9
Sesame seeds: 2 Tablespoons

Method:

Heat 3 Tablespoon of sesame oil in a pan and add the mustard seeds. When they splutter, add the channa dal, asafoetida and the red chillies. Ensure that you have broken four of the red chillies before adding them, as whole chillies when heated, can explode. Add the peanuts and fry well.

Add the turmeric powder, Tamarind concentrate and curry leaves and reduce the heat. Allow the mixture to boil under low heat - when done the oil will float to the top. Remove from fire and add the cooked rice and salt. Mix well - this can be served hot or cold. For a special garnish, dry roast the remaining two red chillies with the sesame seeds. Grind coarsely and then add to the rice. The rice should taste spicy and tangy.

Serve hot with Aubergine Dip and Poppadoms. Tamarind rice also lasts longer than most other food items and can be stored in a cool place for 2-3 days.

Kanu

aubergine thokayal (aubergine dip)

Serves: 4-5
Preparation time: 5 minutes
Cooking time: 40 minutes

Ingredients:

Aubergine: 1 large one
Tamarind Concentrate: 1 Teaspoon
Urad Dal: 1 Tablespoon
Sesame Oil: 1 Tablespoon
Ginger: a small piece (1")
Dry red chillies: 2-3
Asafoetida: ¼ Teaspoon
Chopped Coriander leaves: 3 Tablespoons
Salt: to taste
Sunflower Oil: For deep-frying

Method:

Wash and dry the aubergine. Cut into several large pieces and deep fry on medium heat. Remember that if the oil is too hot, the aubergines will turn brown very quickly but will not cook properly.

Break the red chillies into several pieces. Heat the sesame oil in a pan and add the dal and the chillies to it. When the dal starts to turn brown, add the asafoetida and remove from heat.

Peel and chop the ginger. Grind the ginger and dal mixture to a coarse mix. Add the fried aubergine, Tamarind concentrate, salt and coriander and grind to a smooth paste.

Serve at room temperature - this is a delicious dip and goes well with Poppadoms.

Kanu
lemon rice

Serves: 3-4
Preparation time:
Cooking time: 35 minutes (includes 20 minutes for cooking the rice)

Ingredients:

Cooked Rice: 2 Cups
Peanuts: 2 Tablespoons
Channa Dal: 1 Tablespoon
Curry leaves: 3-4
Sesame Oil: 4 Tablespoons
Turmeric Powder: ¼ Teaspoon
Mustard Seeds: 1 Teaspoon
Asafoetida: ¼ Teaspoon
Lemon juice: 3 Tablespoons
Green Chilli, chopped fine: 1
Salt: To taste

Method:

Add a few drops of sesame oil to the cooked rice and spread out on a plate so that the grains don't stick together. In a pan, heat the oil and add the mustard seeds. When they crackle, add the asafoetida, channa dal, curry leaves and peanuts. Add the green chilli, rice, salt and turmeric powder. Reduce the heat to very low and mix well.

Mixing the rice is an art - my mother taught me how to do it patiently and start from one end of the pan and keep mixing until the rice is uniformly coloured. Add the lemon juice and check the seasoning. You can add more lemon juice if required.

Lemon rice can be served hot or cold and tastes delicious with Poppodums and Tomato Raita.

Kanu

curd rice

Indian Festive Flavours

Serves: 3-4
Preparation time:
Cooking time: 40 minutes (includes 20 minutes for cooking rice)

Ingredients:

Cooked Rice: 2 Cups
Milk: ½ Cup
Plain Yogurt: 2 Cups
Green Chilli, chopped fine: 1
Curry Leaves: 2-3
Cucumber: ¼ of a fruit
Mustard Seeds: 1 Teaspoon
Asafoetida: ¼ Teaspoon
Salt: To taste
Coriander, chopped fine: 1 Tablespoon
Oil: 1 Tablespoon

Method:

Mash the cooked rice well and mix with milk, yogurt and salt. Take care that the rice is not too warm while adding the milk. In a food processor, chop the cucumber really fine. Add this to the rice mix.

In a small pan, heat the oil and add the mustard seeds. When they splutter, add the curry leaves, asafoetida and the green chilli. Add this to the rice and mix well. Garnish with coriander and chill in the fridge. Serve Cold - on its own or with tomato chutney.

tomato raita
(spicy tomato and yogurt sauce)

Serves: 3-4
Preparation time: 5 minutes
Cooking time: 10 minutes

Ingredients:

Tomatoes: 2
Mustard Seeds: 1 Teaspoon
Fenugreek Seeds (Optional): ¼ Teaspoon
Turmeric Powder: ¼ Teaspoon
Asafoetida: a pinch
Yogurt: 3 Cups
Salt: To taste
Sesame or Olive Oil: 1 Tablespoon
Coriander leaves (Optional): For a garnish

Method:

Chop the tomatoes finely and reserve. In a pan, heat the oil and add mustard seeds. When they splutter, add the fenugreek seeds, asafoetida, salt and turmeric powder. Add the tomatoes and stir well on low heat until the tomatoes are well cooked and you can see the oil separating from the mixture. Remove from heat.

Whisk the yogurt and transfer to a serving bowl. Add the tomatoes and stir. Garnish with some coriander leaves. This sauce tastes delicious with a variety of rice-based dishes and is served cold.

okra raita
(ladies finger and yogurt sauce)

Serves: 3-4
Preparation time: 10 minutes
Cooking time: 20 minutes

Ingredients:

Okra/Ladies Fingers: 4-5
Mustard Seeds: 1 Teaspoon
Urad Dal: 1 Teaspoon
Yogurt: 3 Cups
Salt: To taste
Sesame or Olive Oil: 1 Tablespoon
Sunflower Oil: 5 Tablespoons

Method:

Wash and top the Okra. Slice into small round slices and dry on a kitchen napkin. Heat the sunflower oil and deep-fry the Okra until they are crisp and brown. Drain on Kitchen paper and reserve.

In a pan, heat the oil and add mustard seeds. When they splutter, add the urad dal and fry until the dal turns pink. Remove from heat.

Whisk the yogurt, season with salt and transfer to a serving bowl. Just before you are ready to serve, add the fried Okra and the mustard tarka* and stir. This is a delightful side dish that your guests will love.

---

*   See Helpful Hints and Tips for details on Tarka

festivals in february/march

Nombu

There is a very romantic tale about a married couple called Satyavan and Savitri. Satyavan, the husband, was doomed to die young and Savitri married him even though she was fully aware of this. When "Yama", the god of death, came to fetch Satyavan's soul, Savitri followed them to the heavens. Finally, impressed by her perseverance, Yama agreed to grant her a wish. And you guessed it; she tricked him into returning Satyavan back to life by asking for a blessing of many children with Satyavan. During her long trek following Yama, Savitri is said to have prayed to Goddess Ambika. As she had no food to make an offering to the Goddess, Savitri used clay to make "Adai" (a small pancake) as an offering. Nombu is celebrated by making Adais but luckily the main ingredient is rice and not clay.

Ram Navami

Rama was an ancient Hindu King, believed to be an incarnation of "Vishnu", one of the 3 main Hindu gods. Rama was considered pure and righteous and gave up his throne to please his stepmother. His wife, Sita, was kidnapped by an evil King who hid her in his island Kingdom. Rama amassed a variety of followers and built an army that vanquished the King and brought Sita home. There are many festivals celebrated in his honour and this is one of them.

This period also marks the start of the Tamil New year.

sweet adai
(sweet short pancakes)

Serves: 2
Preparation time:
Cooking time: 50 minutes *(assumes you are using a can of black-eyed beans)*

Ingredients:

Rice Powder: 1 Cup
Jaggery*: 1 Cup
Black-eyed beans: 1 Tablespoon
Coconut shavings: 2 Tablespoons

Method:

In a pan, boil 2 Cups of water and add the jaggery. Stir well until it dissolves completely. Add the cooked black-eyed beans and give it a boil. Remove from heat and add the rice powder. Ensure that you mix it well before adding the coconut shavings. The mixture should get the consistency of a thick paste.

On a greased surface, take a small lime-sized ball of this paste and flatten in the form of a 2-inch disc. Make a small hole in the centre using a clean finger. Make discs out of the remaining paste.

In a steamer, steam all the discs for 10 minutes until cooked. The best way to do this is in a pressure cooker, using an "idli-steamer" if you have one.

When cooked, sheen develops on the adais' surface. Cool and serve with white butter.

Note:

1. Idli-steamers are available in Indian shops around the country.

2. It is preferable to use a can of black-eyed beans - alternatively, soak overnight and pressure cook with plenty of water and drain. If you are not using a pressure cooker, boil the beans for at least 30 minutes in plenty of water. Remove a bean and check if it mashes easily to see if it has been cooked well.

---

* You can substitute Jaggery with brown or muscavado sugar. Jaggery is available in the asian shops/section of the supermarkets

salt adai
(savoury short pancakes)

Serves: 2
Preparation time:
Cooking time: 50 minutes *(assumes you are using a can of black-eyed beans)*

Ingredients:

Rice Powder: 1 Cup
Black-eyed beans: 1 Tablespoon
(You can use a can of black-eyed beans - alternatively, soak and pressure-cook with plenty of water and drain)
Coconut shavings: 2 Tablespoons
Mustard seeds: 1 Teaspoon
Channa dal: 1 Tablespoon
Green chillies (chopped fine): 3
Curry leaves (crushed): 1 Tablespoon
Sesame Oil: 4 Teaspoons
Salt: to taste

Method:

Heat the oil in a small pan and add the mustard seeds. When they splutter, add the channa dal, chopped chillies and curry leaves. Let the dal brown for a few seconds. Add 2 Cups of water and ½ Teaspoon of salt and the coconut shavings. When the water boils, add the black-eyed beans, rice powder and remove from heat. Stir well to form a paste.

On a greased surface, take a small lime-sized ball of this paste and flatten in the form of a 2-inch disc. Make a small hole in the centre using a clean finger. Make discs out of the remaining paste.

In a steamer, steam all the discs for 10 minutes until cooked. The best way to do this is in a pressure cooker, using an "idli-steamer" if you have one.

When cooked, sheen develops on the adais' surface. Cool and serve with Kootu.

kalli kootu (vegetable stew)

🕐 🕐

Serves: 3-4
Preparation time: 10-15 minutes
Cooking time: 40 minutes

Ingredients:

Broad beans: 4-5
Raw green banana (small sized): 1
Potato (medium sized): 1
Yellow pumpkin: 25grams
White pumpkin: 25grams
Peas: ½ Cup
Green chillies: 4
Grated coconut: ½ Cup
Turmeric powder: ½ Teaspoon
Mustard seeds: 1 Teaspoon
Split Black Gram: 1 Teaspoon
Curry leaves (crushed): 1 Tablespoon
Coconut Oil: 1 Tablespoon
Rice powder: 2 Teaspoons
Salt: to taste

Method:

Cut all the vegetables into small pieces (about an inch long). Try and keep them to the same shape and size to ensure they cook evenly. In a pan, bring 2 Cups of water to a boil. Add salt, turmeric and all the vegetables and let them cook on low heat.

In the meantime, grind the coconut with the green chillies and a Tablespoon of water. When the vegetables are cooked (test them with a spoon), add the coconut-chilli paste. Add the curry leaves and remove from heat. Sprinkle the rice powder and mix.

In a small pan, heat the coconut oil and add the mustard seeds. When they splutter, add the Split Black Gram. Remove from heat and pour on top of the vegetables. Serve hot with the salt adais.

Note:

You can try various other combinations of vegetables - squashes and courgettes can replace pumpkins and gourds.

Nombu
talakham (sesame vegetable stew)

Serves: 3-4
Preparation time: 10-15 minutes
Cooking time: 40 minutes

Ingredients:

For the Spice powder:
Rice: 2 Tablespoons
Sesame seeds: 1 Teaspoon
Arhar dal: ½ Teaspoon
Split Black Gram: ½ Teaspoon
Asafoetida: a pinch
Red chillies: 2-3

For the Gravy:
Broad Beans: 4-5
Potato (medium sized): 1
Aubergine (small, halved): 1
Yellow pumpkin: 25grams
White pumpkin: 25grams
Peas: ½ Cup
Green chilli (cut in half length-wise): 1
Tamarind concentrate: 1 Teaspoon
Mustard seeds: ½ Teaspoon
Split Black Gram: ½ Teaspoon
Red Chilly (broken into 2): 1
Coconut Oil: 1 Tablespoon
Turmeric powder: ½ Teaspoon
Salt: to taste

Method:

Cut all the vegetables into small pieces (about an inch long). Try and keep them to the same shape and size to ensure they cook evenly.

In a pan, bring 2 Cups of water to a boil. Add Tamarind concentrate, salt, turmeric and all the vegetables and let them cook on low heat.

Dry roast the ingredients of the spice powder and grind in a mixie without any water.

When the veggies are cooked, add the spice powder and mix well.

In a small pan, heat the coconut oil and add the mustard seeds. When they splutter, add the Split Black Gram. Remove from heat and pour on top of the vegetables. Serve hot with boiled rice.

Note:
You can try various other combinations of vegetables - squashes and courgettes can replace pumpkins and gourds.

panakham
(ginger jaggery sherbet)

Serves: 3-4
Preparation time: 20 minutes
Cooking time:

Ingredients:

Jaggery: 75grams
Dry ginger powder: ½ Teaspoon
Cardamom powder: ½ Teaspoon

Method:

Soak the Jaggery in 5 Cups of warm water until it dissolves. Pass this mix through a coarse sieve to remove any remaining lumps. Add the ginger and cardamom powders and mix well. Serve chilled as a cold drink.

Note:

If you cannot find Jaggery, substitute it with brown cane sugar

Ram Navami

neer moru
(spicy buttermilk)

Serves: 3
Preparation time: 10 minutes
Cooking time:

Ingredients:

Butter milk: 3 glasses
Green chilly: 1
Curry leaves: 2 Teaspoons
Ginger (fresh): ½" piece
Salt: to taste

Method:

Grind the green chilli and ginger and mix with the buttermilk, salt and curry leaves. Using an eggbeater or a mixie, churn well. Serve cold.

An alternate method is to omit the green chillies and ginger and just add the curry leaves and salt to the buttermilk. Add a Tablespoon of lemon juice and churn. This buttermilk is less spicy.

vadai paruppu
(mango mung salad)

⏱

Serves: 2-3
Preparation time: 1 hour
Cooking time: 15 minutes

Ingredients:

Mung dal: 1 Cup
Cucumber: ½
Green chilli: 1
Mustard seeds: ½ Teaspoon
Raw Mango: ½
Curry leaves: 1 Tablespoon
Lemon juice: 1 Tablespoon
Sesame Oil or Sunflower Oil: 1 Tablespoon

Method:

Soak the Mung Dal for one hour. You can cook the Dal very lightly in boiling water and drain. The Dal should still be whole and crisp. Chop the cucumber and Mango into very small pieces. In a pan, heat the oil and add the mustard seeds and curry leaves. When they splutter, remove from heat and add to the Dal. Mix in with the cucumber, mango, lemon juice and finely chopped, de-seeded green chilli.

This is served as a small side salad and tastes wonderful as a topping on crisp bread.

festivals in august

Janmashtami

Krishna is probably the most famous of the Hindu gods - and we celebrate his birthday this month. My mother used to draw little feet out of rice-flour paste from the doorway of the house, all the way into the kitchen, to signify the steps that a little Krishna would take. So, the expectation was that little Krishna would enter the house and make his way straight to the delicacies that would be made for him that day.

All the young children in the colony would get together and decorate a tableaux depicting various scenes of the mythology surrounding Krishna's birth (similar to a nativity scene) and then finally get to eat the goodies made that day. Krishna was supposed to be very fond of flaked rice and I have given a couple of recipes using this. Flaked rice is easily available in the Asian section of most supermarkets.

Ganesh Chaturti

Ganesh, the elephant god is another well known Hindu god. Ganesh Chaturti celebrates his birthday and normally occurs between the end of August and mid- September, based on the Hindu calendar. Ganesh is believed to be very fond of sweets and cannot resist the delicious modak. On this day, my mother used to make an absolutely stunning array of eatables, which were offered to the god before being consumed by the family.

seedai
(fried savoury dumpling)

🕐🕐🕐

Serves: 4-6
Preparation time: 30 minutes (assumes the use of Rice flour)
Cooking time: 50 minutes

Ingredients:

Raw Rice: 3 Cups
(You can use 3 Cups of Rice Flour instead)
Grated fresh coconut: 1 Cup
(You can substitute with 3 Tablespoon desiccated coconut)
Asafoetida powder: ¼ Teaspoon
Cumin seeds: ½ Teaspoon
Black pepper coarsely ground: ½ Teaspoon
Urad Dal powder: 2 Tablespoons
White sesame seeds: 1 Teaspoon
Salt: to taste
Oil: for deep-frying

Method:

If you're using raw rice, then soak in water for at least 2 hours and drain on a kitchen towel. When dry, grind and sieve to produce a fine powder. Alternatively, use fresh rice flour from the shops. Heat a pan on gentle heat and add the flour – fry lightly until you can see the steam just rising. Remove from the heat; add the rest of the ingredients except the oil. With very little water, make stiff dough. Roll the dough into tiny balls (the size of a marble).

Heat the oil to a moderate temperature (not smoking) and fry batches of the Seedai balls until they are golden brown in colour. Remove one from the oil and break to check if cooked. If it breaks easily, it is ready. Remove from the oil, drain and serve once they are cooled down.

This recipe is given a high difficulty level as it takes a lot of patience to roll the dough into many small, evenly sized balls and then to deep-fry them correctly. For those who are endowed with patience as a virtue (and you may have guessed that I am not), this is a relatively easy recipe.

sweet seedai
(fried sweet dumpling)

🕐🕐🕐
Serves: 4-6
Preparation time:
Cooking time: 1 hour

Ingredients:

Rice Flour: 3 Cups
Jaggery/Muscovado Sugar: 2 ¼ Cups
Cardamom powder: ¼ Teaspoon
Desiccated Coconut: 2 Tablespoons
Sesame Seeds: 1 Tablespoon
Urad Dal Powder: 2 Tablespoons
Oil: for deep-frying

Method:

Heat the sugar/jaggery in a pan with very little water until it completely dissolves. Add the coconut. When the syrup becomes thick enough to roll into balls, remove from the heat and add the rice flour and mix well. Add the Cardamom and Sesame seeds and the Urad Dal powder to make well-mixed dough.

Roll into tiny cherry sized spheres and deep fry in small batches, over low heat.

This recipe is given a high difficulty level as it takes a lot of patience to roll the dough into many small, evenly sized balls and then to deep-fry them correctly. For those who are endowed with patience as a virtue (and you may have guessed that I am not), this is a relatively easy recipe.

thattai
(crunchy rice and dal savoury snack)

🕐🕐🕐

Serves: 4-6
Preparation time: 1.5 hours
Cooking time: 40 minutes

Ingredients:

Rice Flour: 3 Cups
Urad Dal Powder: 3 Teaspoons
Butter: 2 Tablespoons
Urad Dal: 1 Teaspoon
Channa Dal: 1 Teaspoon
Curry Leaves: 8 - 10
Paprika or Red Chilli Powder: 2 Teaspoons
Asafoetida: ¼ Teaspoon
Salt: To taste
Sunflower Oil: for deep-frying

Method:

Soak the Urad and Channa Dal for an hour and drain. Mix all the ingredients and add a little water and mix to get fine pliable dough.

Spread a dry clean kitchen towel on a table. Using wet hands roll out a small ball of dough into a pancake (around 3 inches in diameter). As the pancakes don't have to be very thin, you can use your hands instead of a rolling pin. Shape all the dough into pancakes. Heat the oil to moderate heat - if it starts smoking, it is too hot. Deep-fry all the pancakes by gently lowering them one by one into the oil. It is important that the oil is not too hot and not cool; otherwise the pancakes will not cook properly. Serve cold.

Note:

If you cannot find Urad Dal flour in the shops then gently dry roast the dal until pink and cool. Grind in a coffee grinder to a fine powder.

Once again, this recipe takes a great deal of patience to get all the pancakes rolled out to the same size and thickness. It is not difficult - just time consuming.

sweet modak
(steamed coconut dumplings)

Serves: 4-6
Preparation time:
Cooking time: 1 hour 15 minutes

Ingredients:

Filling:
Grated Coconut: 1 Cup
Jaggery: 1 Cup
Cardamom powder: ¼ Teaspoon
Channa Dal (Optional): ½ Cup
Ghee: 1 Tablespoon

For the Dumpling shell:
Rice Flour: 2 Cups
Sesame Seeds: 2 Teaspoons
Salt: a pinch
Sunflower/Sesame Oil 1 Tablespoon

Method:
For the filling:
Cook the Channa Dal until very soft. Mash into a paste. Melt the jaggery in a pan, with a couple of tablespoons of water. Add the grated coconut and ghee. Stir continuously on low heat and add the Cardamom powder and Channa Dal mash. Stir until the mixture is thick. Cool and rollout small balls of filling.

For the Shell:
In a pan, heat 3 Cups of water. As it starts to boil, add the Sesame seeds, oil and salt. Stir in the rice flour making sure that lumps are not formed. Continue to stir until the mixture leaves the sides of the pan. Remove from heat and cover, leaving the mix to cool.

Using oiled hands, knead the cooled dough well. Taking around a Tablespoon of the mix at a time, pat this into a disk (3 inches in diameter). Place a filling ball in the centre of the disk and bring the ends together to form a dumpling. Repeat with the rest of the dough.

Place all the modaks on a greased steamer plate and steam for around 8 minutes until done.

Serve warm - they taste delicious both warm and cold.

Note:
You can make the filling without the Channa dal - however the dal serves as a binding agent and makes healthier fillings.

savoury urad modak (steamed savoury dumplings)

⏲ ⏲ ⏲

Serves: 4
Preparation time: 1 hour 10 minutes
Cooking time: 1 hour

Ingredients:

Urad Dal: 2 Cups
Green Chillies: 2
Red Chillies: 1
Salt: To Taste
Asafoetida powder: ¼ Teaspoon
Fresh Coriander: 1 Tablespoon
Grated Coconut: 1 Tablespoon
Mustard Seeds: 1 Teaspoon
Sesame Oil: 1 Tablespoon

For the Dumpling shell:
Rice Flour: 2 Cups
Sesame Seeds: 2 Teaspoons
Salt: a pinch
Sunflower/Sesame Oil 1 Tablespoon

Method:
For the Filling:

Soak the Urad Dal for an hour. Chop and deseed the green chillies. Grind the drained dal with the chillies, salt and asafoetida, with a little water to form a coarse paste. Put this mixture on a greased steamer and steam for 6-7 minutes. In a pan, heat the oil and add the mustard seeds. When they splutter, add the steamed dal mixture and mix well. Add the coconut and coriander and remove from heat. Roll into balls of filling.

For the Shell:

In a pan, heat 3 Cups of water. As it starts to boil, add the Sesame seeds, oil and salt. Stir in the rice flour making sure that lumps are not formed. Continue to stir until the mixture leaves the sides of the pan. Remove from heat and cover, leaving the mix to cool.

Using oiled hands, knead the cooled dough well. Taking around a Tablespoon of the mix at a time, pat this into a disk (3 inches in diameter). Place a filling ball in the centre of the disk and bring the ends together to form a dumpling. Repeat with the rest of the dough.

Place all the modaks on a greased steamer plate and steam for around 8 minutes until done. Serve warm with Tomato Chutney - delicious!

Although this is given a "Difficult" rating, believe me, the end result is well worth the trouble!

tomato chutney

🕐
Serves: 3-4
Preparation time: 5 minutes
Cooking time: 30 minutes

Ingredients:

Tomatoes: 6
Mustard Seeds: 1 Teaspoon
Fenugreek Seeds (Optional): 1 Teaspoon
Sesame or Olive Oil: 3 Tablespoons
Salt: To taste
Asafoetida: a pinch
Chilli powder: ½ Teaspoon
Turmeric powder: ¼ Teaspoon

Method:

Wash and chop the tomatoes finely. In a saucepan heat the oil and add the mustard seeds when hot. As the seeds splutter, add the fenugreek seeds and chopped tomatoes. Mix in the salt, chilli and turmeric powders and asafoetida and cook over low heat for at least 15-20 minutes, stirring regularly.

The tomatoes mash down nicely and come together in the pan - the water evaporates and you know the chutney is ready when the oil separates out from the tomatoes.

The chutney can be stored in the fridge for a few days and is one of the most delicious tomato preparations.

festivals in september, october, and november

Navarathri (September)

Navarathri literally means "9 nights" and it is a festival that spans for 9 days and nights. This was one of the highlights of the year for me as we used to celebrate by building up tableaux of dolls. We were wildly creative and our tableaux ranged from mythological Hindu stories to weddings, cricket matches and even a sports complex. We'd even weave current events or political satire into the displays. We'd have a huge range of visitors through this period and it was tradition for the South Indian ladies to sing - not dissimilar to the tradition of Christmas carols!

All the ladies were welcomed and were given a farewell gift, comprising of a coconut, betel leaves, fruit and "Prasad" or a food offering to the gods. Some of my nicest childhood memories are about these celebrations. The Prasad or offering would differ each day - and I have included only 2 of the possible recipes.

Deepavali/Diwali (October/November)

Deepavali or Diwali, as it's commonly called, is one of the most well-known and widely celebrated Hindu Festivals. Deepavali literally means the "Festival of Lights". There are many mythological stories surrounding why Diwali is actually celebrated. All of them revolve around the triumph of good over evil. One of the myths is that on this day, the good King Rama returned to his kingdom after winning a war against the evil King Ravana, who had kidnapped his wife. On the night of his return, there was no moon in the sky and Rama's subjects lit up the entire kingdom with lamps to dispel the darkness and to welcome the King and Queen. Another myth is that Diwali is celebrated as the day when the god Krishna fought against a demon Narakasura and defeated him.

While North-Indians celebrate Diwali at night, the Tamil Deepavali is celebrated in the early hours of the morning. The one thing I always dreaded was being woken up by my mother at 4 a.m., to then have an "oil-bath" with special spiced oil she prepared for the festival. But after that, it used to be great fun - we got to wear new clothes, pray, and then go out to play with fireworks. That was the most exciting bit - I never liked fireworks that went bang - but loved pretty (and silent) firework displays and rockets that would light up the morning sky.

Traditionally, we ate "Palaharam" in the morning - one of the several recipes that follow. Other snacks were also served through the day. Diwali is one of the nicest and most social festivals, as people would go out to meet family and friends. All guests were served delicacies and sweets and people always exchanged gifts. In the evening, we would light oil lamps or candles outside the house. The 2 days after Diwali are also celebrated as smaller festivals in the North.

I have given a variety of recipes for the festival - my mother did not make all of them every year - but we always got to eat a lovely selection from these. I hope you enjoy them as much as I do.

Navarathri
sundal (chickpea stir-fry)

34

Indian Festive Flavours

Serves: 2
Preparation time:
Cooking time: 10 minutes (assumes you are using a can of chickpeas)

Ingredients:

Chick Peas: 1 Can
Grated fresh coconut: 2 Tablespoons
(You can substitute with 1 Tablespoon dry coconut)
Asafoetida powder: ¼ Teaspoon
Mustard seeds: ½ Teaspoon
Coconut Oil: 2 Tablespoons
Curry leaves: 3-4
Green Chillies: 1
Salt: to taste

Method:

If you are using a can of chickpeas, simply drain and wash. If you are using dried chickpeas, you must soak them overnight and pressure-cook until soft. I would recommend a can - but choose one that has no added salt or sugar.

In a pan, heat the coconut oil. When it almost starts smoking, add the mustard seeds and let them splutter. Add the Asafoetida and curry leaves and green chilli, chopped fine. Add the chickpeas, salt and cook in low heat for 5 minutes.

Add the grated coconut and serve as a snack.

Note:

Black-eyed beans, Split yellow peas, or fresh green peas can substitute the chickpeas. If you are using green peas, substitute the green chilli with a dried red chilli broken in half.

Navarathri

vella sundal (bean pudding)

Serves: 2
Preparation time: 5 minutes
Cooking time: 20 minutes

Ingredients:

Aduki Beans: 1 can
Jaggery/Muscovado Sugar: 2 Tablespoons
Grated Fresh Coconut: 1 Tablespoon
Cardamom Powder: ½ Teaspoon
Ghee: 1 Tablespoon

Method:

Drain and wash the Aduki Beans. If you're using jaggery, use a food processor to break into tiny pieces. Heat the jaggery/sugar with a little bit of water to form sugar syrup. Add the beans, coconut and cardamom. Add the ghee and mix well. Serve warm.

This can convert into a lovely dessert by adding a dollop of double cream on top.

Diwali

idli (steamed rice cakes)

🕐

Serves: 4-6
Preparation time: 3 hours + 12 hours fermenting time
Cooking time: 20 minutes

Ingredients:

Urad Dal: 1 Cup
Parboiled Rice: 4 Cups
Salt: To taste

Method:

Wash and soak the Rice and Dal overnight (or for at least 3 hours). Drain and grind to a smooth paste along with the salt. Leave the batter to ferment in a covered dish overnight. Make sure that the dish is large enough for the batter to more than double in volume.

Pour a spoonful of batter into every mould of an Idli-steamer and steam for 10 minutes. After 10 minutes, reduce the heat, remove the lid while carefully avoiding the steam and insert a knife inside one of the Idlis to check if it's done. If there's no batter sticking to the knife, the Idlis are cooked. If not, replace the lid and steam for another 2-3 minutes.

Serve hot with Coconut Chutney and Sambar.

Note:

1. Idli-steamers are available in Indian shops around the country. If you cannot find these, use small metallic poaching cups to hold the batter and steam these.

2. If you cannot find parboiled rice, you can use ordinary rice. Just warm ordinary raw rice in a pan and then soak it.

3. You can also get ready-made Idli mix in the supermarkets. You can get delicious Idlis with minimal effort. It also cuts out the time to prepare and ferment the batter.

Diwali

dosa (rice pancakes)

Serves: 4-6
Preparation time: 8 hours (including fermenting time)
Cooking time: 20-30 minutes

Ingredients:

Batter:
Urad Dal: ¾ Cup
Parboiled Rice: 4 Cups
Salt: To taste
Oil: 2-3 Tablespoons

Method:
Soak the Rice and Dal in warm water for at least 3 hours. Drain and grind to a very smooth paste. Add the salt and leave to ferment for at least 4 hours. Make sure that the dish you leave the batter in is big enough for the batter to expand to nearly double its volume. In the meantime, make your choice of filling (given in the next page).

Heat a pancake pan (Tava) on medium heat and spread a Tablespoon of oil all over it. Ladle out 2 spoons of the batter in the centre and spread quickly to make a thin pancake. You can pour a few drops of oil around the outside of the pancake to help it cook quicker. Keep the heat low as otherwise the batter will stick to the pan. When done,

you can see the sides of the pancake rising up from the pan slightly and you should be able to slide a Flat pancake-flip underneath the Dosa and flip over to the other side. Cook the other side in the same way. Remove from heat. Add a spoonful of filling (either 1 or 2) in the centre and fold the Dosa into a crescent shape. Serve warm with Sambar, Coconut Chutney and Gunpowder. You can also serve a plain Dosa - it tastes just as delicious.

You don't have to finish the batter in a day. Excess batter can be stored in the fridge for a few days or frozen. If you are freezing the batter, make sure you defrost it thoroughly by leaving it out before using it and making sure it has warmed up to room temperature. Cold batter will not make good pancakes.

Diwali

dosa fillings

Indian Festive Flavours

🕐

Serves: 3-4
Preparation time: 10 minutes (both fillings)
Cooking time: 30 minutes (Filling1); 20 minutes (Filling2)

Ingredients:

Filling 1- Potato:
  Boiled Potatoes: 3-4 medium-sized
  Red Onion: 1
  Green Chilli: 1
  Mustard Seeds: 1 Teaspoon
  Channa Dal: 1 Teaspoon
  Curry Leaves: 2-3
  Fresh Coriander: 1 Tablespoon, Chopped
  Sesame Oil: 1 Tablespoon
  Turmeric Powder: ¼ Teaspoon
  Salt: To Taste
  Lemon juice: 1 Tablespoon

Filling 2 - Salsa:
  Red Onions: 3
  Tomatoes: 6
  Green Chilli: 1
  Mustard Seeds: 1 Teaspoon
  Cumin Seeds: 1 Teaspoon
  Fresh Coriander: 2 Tablespoons, Chopped
  Sesame Oil: 1 Tablespoon
  Turmeric Powder: ¼ Teaspoon
  Salt: To Taste

Method - Filling 1:

Mash the potatoes well - you can remove the skin if you like, but I retain the skin as this is the most nutritious bit of the vegetable. Chop the onion and chilli finely. Heat the oil in a pan and add the mustard seeds. When they splutter, add the channa dal and curry leaves. Once the dal is brown, add the chilli and fry for a minute. Add the onion and fry until the onion is just turning brown. Add the mashed potatoes, salt and turmeric powder and mix well. Leave this to cook for 5 minutes, stirring frequently. Add the lemon juice and remove from heat. Add the coriander leaves and mix well. The filling should not be totally dry. If it looks too dry, add 2 Tablespoon of water and warm through.

Method - Filling 2:

Chop the onions and green chillies finely. Chop the tomatoes and retain the juices. In a pan, heat the oil and add the mustard seeds. When the splutter, add the cumin seeds. Add the green chilli and fry for a minute. Add the onions and fry until they start turning brown. Add the tomatoes, turmeric powder and salt and cook over low heat until the tomatoes have reduced down considerably. Add the fresh coriander and remove from heat.

Fill the Dosa just before serving - otherwise, it can get soggy.

Diwali

gunpowder (sesame chilli chutney)

Serves: 6-8
Preparation time:
Cooking time: 30 minutes

Ingredients:

Dry Red Chilli: 50 grams
Channa Dal: 3 Tablespoons
Urad Dal: 3 ½ Tablespoons
Asafoetida: 1 Teaspoon
Sesame seeds (white): 4 Tablespoons
Salt: to taste
Sesame Oil: 1 Tablespoon /serving

Method:

Heat a pan and add the Channa Dal. Stir over low heat until the dal turn pink. Repeat with the Urad Dal - add Asafoetida to this and stir until it turns pink. Remove the pan from heat. Add the chillies to the warm pan and stir for 3-4 minutes. The reason one adds the chillies after removing the pan from heat is to prevent the chillies from giving a strong scent while being heated and making everyone in the vicinity sneeze. Add the salt to this mix and grind to a fine powder.

Heat the pan again and dry roast the sesame seeds until pink in colour. Grind the sesame separately and mix with the rest of the powdered spices.

Store in an airtight container. When you are ready to serve the chutney, take 2 Tablespoon of powder and add 1 Tablespoon of sesame oil and mix well. A word of warning - this can be very spicy and needs to be used sparingly. So, try not serving more than 1 Teaspoon of chutney at a time.

Note:

The Dals are warmed up separately as they are of different sizes and will not brown up uniformly if heated together.

aloo bonda (potato croquets)

🕐🕐

Serves: 3-4
Preparation time:
Cooking time: 50 minutes

Ingredients:

For the Filling:
Boiled Potatoes: 3-4 medium-sized
Red Onion: 1
Green Chilli: 1
Mustard Seeds: 1 Teaspoon
Channa Dal: 1 Teaspoon
Curry Leaves: 2-3
Fresh Coriander: 1Tablespoon Chopped
Sesame Oil: 1 Tablespoon
Turmeric Powder: ¼ Teaspoon
Salt: To Taste
Lemon juice: 1 Tablespoon

For the Batter:
Gram Flour: 2 Cups
Asafoetida: ¼ Teaspoon
Chilli Powder: ½ Teaspoon
Salt: To Taste
Sunflower Oil: For Deep frying

Method:

The method of making the bonda filling is similar to Filling 1 of the Dosa, given earlier.

Mash the potatoes well - you can remove the skin if you like, but I retain the skin as this is the most nutritious bit of the vegetable. Chop the onion and chilli finely. Heat the oil in a pan and add the mustard seeds. When they splutter, add the channa dal and curry leaves. Once the dal is brown, add the chilli and fry for a minute. Add the onion and fry until the onion is just turning brown. Add the mashed potatoes, salt and turmeric powder and mix well. Leave this to cook for 5 minutes, stirring frequently. Add the lemon juice and remove from heat. Add the coriander leaves and mix well. Leave to cool.

When cooler, roll out small balls of the potato mix (the size of a small plum).

Prepare the batter by sifting and mixing the gram flour with all the other ingredients except the oil. Add a little water to make a batter that is thin enough to be spooned but not very watery.

Heat the oil in a deep pan. Drop the potato balls in the batter mix. When the oil is hot, deep-fry the balls in batches. When they turn golden-brown in colour, drain on to kitchen paper.

Serve hot with Tomato Chutney.

Diwali

sambar (spiced lentil soup)

🕐🕐

Serves: 4
Preparation time: 1 hour
Cooking time: 40 minutes

Ingredients:

For the paste:
Coriander Seeds: 2 Teaspoons
Channa Dal: 1 Teaspoon
Fenugreek Seeds: 3-4
Asafoetida: ¼ Teaspoon
Dried Red Chillies: 3
Sesame Oil: 1 Tablespoon
Grated Coconut: 1 Tablespoon

For the gravy:
Tamarind Concentrate: 1 Teaspoon
Shallots or baby onions: 4-5
Mustard Seeds: 1 Teaspoon
Arhar Dal: ½ Cup
Curry leaves: 3-4
Turmeric powder: ¼ Teaspoon
Tomato: 1/2
Fresh Coriander (chopped): 1 Tablespoon
Salt: To taste
Sesame Oil: 1 Tablespoon

Method:

To make the paste, heat the sesame oil and add the coriander and Fenugreek seeds and dal. Fry for 2 minutes and add the red chillies and asafoetida. When the chillies start turning brown, remove from heat. Once cooled, grind with 2 Tablespoon of water and the coconut to form a fine paste. Keep aside.

Soak the Dal for an hour and cook with a little salt and turmeric powder until the Dal has lost its shape and can be easily mashed. Peel the shallots - if they are big, halve them. In a saucepan, heat the sesame oil and add the mustard seeds. When they splutter, add the shallots. Stir the shallots well and fry them until they are evenly browned. Add 3 Cups of water, Tamarind concentrate, curry leaves, tomato and salt and bring to a boil. Reduce the heat and let the mixture bubble away for 10 minutes. Add the dal and the paste and stir well. When the Sambar starts boiling again, remove from heat and garnish with fresh coriander.

Note:

An alternate method of making the Sambar is to buy readymade Sambar-powder from the supermarket. If you are doing this, there is no need to make the paste. Simply add a Tablespoon of Sambar powder to the water at the same time as you add the tamarind and follow the rest of the recipe.

rava upma
(savoury semolina porridge)

Serves: 2-3
Preparation time: 5 minutes
Cooking time: 15 minutes

Ingredients:

Semolina: 1 Cup
Mustard Seeds: 1 Teaspoon
Channa Dal: 1 Tablespoon
Asafoetida: ¼ Teaspoon
Green Chilli: 1
Ginger (grated): 1 Teaspoon
Curry leaves: 3-4
Fresh Coriander (chopped): 1 Tablespoon
Ghee or Sesame Oil: 2 Tablespoon
Salt: To Taste

Method:

Chop the green chilli finely. Heat the ghee or oil in a saucepan and add the mustard seeds. When they splutter, add the dal, asafoetida and curry leaves and fry till the dal is brown. Add the green chilli and ginger and fry for another minute.

Add 2 Cups of water and salt and bring to a boil. Reduce the heat and slowly add the semolina, stirring continuously so that lumps are not formed. Cook until the water evaporates and the semolina comes together away from the sides of the pan. Keep stirring regularly. Remove from heat, garnish with coriander and serve hot with chutney and Sambar.

Note:

To make the Upma more colourful and nutritious:

Add half a red onion chopped fine to the Upma along with the chilli and ginger. Add a Tablespoon of grated carrot to the water before adding the semolina.

Diwali

43

Note:

The following 4 snacks will require a special chakli mould - you can buy this mould from some Indian cook shops. You may be able to use a noodle or pasta mould if you are unable to find this.

🕐🕐🕐

Serves: 4-6
Preparation time: 15 minutes
Cooking time: 40 minutes

Ingredients:

Urad Dal Flour: 1 Cup
Rice Flour: 4 Cups
Cumin: 1 Teaspoon
Asafoetida: ¼ Teaspoon
White unsalted butter: 1 Tablespoon
Salt: To Taste
Sunflower Oil: For Deep Frying

Method:
Urad Dal flour can be made at home by roasting the dry dal over low heat until you can start smelling the dal; and then grinding it. Remove from heat before it turns pink and grind and sieve to give you fine flour.

Mix all the ingredients except the oil along with a little water and knead to form dough.

Heat the oil. Take a Chakli Mould and grease it inside with a little oil. Fill it with the dough and squeeze gently into the hot oil in a circular motion. The pipes should fall on top of each other (like spaghetti). Reduce the heat and cook slowly. Turn it over with a slotted spoon and cook until both sides are golden brown. Repeat with the rest of the dough.

Drain onto kitchen paper and store in an airtight container when cooled. This snack can be kept for a week and tastes absolutely delicious as a teatime snack.

Diwali

oma podi
(crispy noodles with carrom seeds)

🕐🕐🕐
Serves: 4-6
Preparation time: 1 hour 15 minutes
Cooking time: 40 minutes

Ingredients:

Gram Flour: 2 Cups
Rice Flour: ½ Cup
Carom Seeds: 1 Teaspoon
White Unsalted Butter: 1 Tablespoon
Salt: To taste
Sunflower Oil: For Deep Frying

Method:

Soak the Carrom seeds in 1 Tablespoon of warm water for an hour. Filter the solution through a tea strainer and discard the seeds. Add the Carrom water to the flour, butter and salt and mix with water to form soft dough. If the dough is very stiff, you will find it hard to pipe the noodles into the oil.

Heat the oil in a deep pan. When hot, reduce the heat. The chakli mould comes with a variety of plates - use one that has pin-sized holes. Fill the mould with the paste and pipe gently into the hot oil in circular motion.

Deep fry on both sides until golden. As the noodles are very fine, this will cook very quickly - make sure the oil is not too hot or it will burn the noodles. Repeat with the rest of the dough.

Cool and store in an airtight container. This will last for a week -if you can keep your hands off it. We finish ours within the next 2 days.

mullu tenguyal or chakli (crunchy sesame pipes)

🕐🕐🕐

Serves: 4-6
Preparation time: 15 minutes
Cooking time: 40 minutes

Ingredients:

Channa Dal: 3/4 Cup
Mung Dal: 1/4 Cup
Urad Dal: ½ Teaspoon
Rice Flour: 3 Cups
Salt: To Taste
Sesame Seeds (white): 1 Tablespoon
Unsalted Butter: 1/2 Tablespoon
Sunflower Oil: For Deep frying

Method:

Dry roast the Channa and Mung Dal and remove from heat before they change colour. Dry roast the Urad dal until it turns pink. Cool all the dals and grind and sieve to produce fine dal flour.

Mix the Dal flour with the rest of the ingredients except the oil to form stiff dough, with a little water. Use the plate with star-shaped holes in the chakli mould. Grease the mould inside with very little oil and fill with the dough.

Heat the oil for deep-frying. When hot, reduce the heat and pipe the Chakli gently into the hot oil, in circular motion. Fry both sides until golden brown and drain onto kitchen paper. Repeat with the rest of the dough.

This is a wonderfully crunchy savoury snack and can be stored in an airtight container for a week.

ribbon pakoda
(spicy ribbons)

🕐🕐🕐
Serves: 4-6
Preparation time: 10 minutes
Cooking time: 40 minutes

Ingredients:

Rice Flour: 3 Cups
Gram Flour: 1 Cup
Red Chilli Powder/Paprika: 1 Teaspoon
White Sesame seeds: ½ Teaspoon
Asafoetida: ¼ Teaspoon
White unsalted butter: 1 Tablespoon
Salt: To Taste
Sunflower Oil: For Deep Frying

Method:

Sift and mix all the ingredients except the oil, with a little water to form soft dough. Heat the oil for deep-frying. Use the plate with slits for the chakli mould and grease inside with a little oil.

Pipe ribbons in a circular motion gently over hot oil and fry both sides until golden brown. Drain on to kitchen paper. Repeat with the rest of the dough.

This is a spicy and crunchy savoury snack - it can be stored in an airtight container for a week.

Note:

Be careful to wash your hands after mixing the dough due as the red chilli powder can cause irritation.

Ribbon Pakoda can also be made without the mould. Roll it out on a flour-dusted surface and cut out strips, just like pasta. You can then fry these strips.

Diwali Sweets
rava burfi (semolina fudge)

Indian Festive Flavours

🕐🕐
Serves: 4-6
Preparation time:
Cooking time: 1 hour

Ingredients:

Semolina: 1 Cup
Ghee: 2 Cups
Milk: 3 Cups
Sugar: 3 ¼ Cups

Method:

Heat a deep pan and add all the ingredients to it. Keep stirring regularly and cook slowly over low heat until the liquid evaporates and mixture leaves the sides of the pan.

Grease a plate or a pan that has a rim and therefore can hold the liquid in place. Pour the mix into the greased plate and spread across the plate. When cool, use a sharp knife and cut the fudge up into small squares.

Note:

You can adjust the sugar as per your taste. Indian sweets do tend to be fairly sweet.

Diwali Sweets
badam burfi (almond fudge)

🕐🕑
Serves: 4-6
Preparation time: Overnight
Cooking time: 1 hour

Ingredients:

Almonds: 1 Cup
Sugar: 1 ½ Cups
Ghee: ¼ Cup
Milk: 3 Tablespoons

Method:

Soak the almonds overnight in warm water. Peel the skin and grind the almonds to a smooth paste with the milk.

Heat a deep pan and add the ghee, sugar and enough water to immerse the sugar. Stir regularly - you can check the syrup for readiness by dipping a spoon in it and pulling it out. If you can see a thread of syrup, it is ready. Add the almond paste to the sugar syrup and reduce the heat. Stir the mix continuously. When the mix starts to leave the sides of the pan, remove from heat.

Grease a plate/pan with a rim with ghee or butter and pour the fudge into it. When cool, use a sharp knife and cut the fudge into small square pieces.

Diwali Sweets
ma ladoo (dal and dry fruit balls)

🕐 🕑

Serves: 4-6
Preparation time: 15 minutes
Cooking time: 30 minutes

Ingredients:

Channa Dal: 2 Cups
White powdered sugar: 2 Cups
Cashew nuts, chopped roughly: ½ Cup
Raisins: 2 Tablespoons
Cardamom Powder: ¼ Teaspoon
Ghee: 2 Cups

Method:

Dry roast the Channa Dal until it turns red in colour. Cool and grind and sieve to form fine dal flour. Mix the flour with the powdered sugar, nuts, raisins and cardamom powder.

Melt the ghee and cool. Take small portions of the flour mixture and add enough ghee to it to form a small round ladoo (or ball). Roll out all the mixture, using a little ghee each time. There should be sufficient ghee in the ladoos so that they don't crumble as soon as you touch them.

festival in december

Kaartikai

The festival of Kaartikai also has the all very familiar custom of lighting lamps. I think Diwali and Kaartikai were part of an ancient ruse to bring some festive cheer in the colder and darker months.

This was celebrated on a full-moon night where prayers were offered to the goddess by lighting oil lamps inside and outside the house. The offerings on the day consisted of 3 types of sweets and a savoury lentil pancake called Paruppu Adai (one of my favourites).

My mother would draw beautiful designs on the floor of the doorway. They are called "Kolam" and are a typical Tamil feature. Traditionally, they are designs made on the ground with rice flour and every house would have a new Kolam drawn in front of the main door each morning. My mother preferred a more permanent solution and her works of art were painted on the floor. I'd help decorate the Kolams with lamps and flowers and they looked fabulous in the evening.

vella pori (sweet puffed rice)/ aval pori (sweet flaked rice)

Serves: 3-4
Preparation time:
Cooking time: 50 minutes

Ingredients:

Puffed Rice: 100 grams
Jaggery: 30 grams
Powdered Ginger: 1 Teaspoon
Powdered Cardamom: 1 Teaspoon
Coconut shavings: 2 Tablespoons

Method:

In a heavy-bottomed pan, boil water and dissolve the jaggery. In very low heat, continue stirring until the jaggery caramelises into thick syrup. Add the rest of the ingredients and mix thoroughly.

Remove from heat and cool the mixture. With oiled hands, roll the rice into large balls of puffed rice. Dig in!

Aval Pori (Sweet Flaked Rice)
Simply replace the puffed rice with flaked rice and follow the steps above.

neyappam
(banana and jaggery dumpling)

Serves: 3-4
Preparation time:
Cooking time: 50 minutes

Ingredients:

Rice Flour: 2 Cups
Jaggery: 1 Cup
Powdered Cardamom: 1 Teaspoon
Coconut Shavings: 1 Tablespoon
Ripe Banana: 1
Ghee: 3 Cups

Method:

Heat ½ Cup of water and dissolve the Jaggery in it. Mash the banana and mix the jaggery, rice flour, cardamom and coconut shavings to form a smooth, thick batter.

Heat the ghee over low heat - test whether the ghee is ready for frying by first trying with a small spoon of batter - it should rise up to top immediately if the oil is hot enough. Carefully, using two tablespoons to drop the batter in the ghee, fry the Neyappams until they are evenly browned. They would only get cooked right through inside if fried over low heat.

Traditionally, Neyappams are cooked in a cast iron vessel called Appa-Kaaral. As this is not easily available, I would suggest the use of any deep frying pan or Karai.

The Neyappams can be warmed in the microwave before serving and taste great with a dollop of fresh cream.

paruppu adai
(spicy lentil pancake)

Indian Festive Flavours

🕐🕐

Serves: 3-4
Preparation time: 4 hours or Overnight
Cooking time: 40 minutes

Ingredients:

Urad Dal: 1/2 Cup
Channa Dal: 1/2 Cup
Arhar Dal: 1/2 Cup
Rice: 1 ½ Cups
Green Chillies: 2
Dried Red Chillies: 2
Asafoetida: ¼ Teaspoon
Salt: to taste
Fresh Coriander (chopped): 1 Tablespoon
Finely chopped Red Onion (Optional): 2 Tablespoons
Finely chopped Cabbage (Optional): 2 Tablespoons
Ghee or Sesame Oil: ½ Cup

Method:

Soak the Dals and Rice overnight in cold water. If short of time, soak them in hot water for at least 4 hours. Drain and grind with all the ingredients except the Optional items (if using). Add just enough water to make a grainy but thick batter. Now add the finely chopped onion or cabbage if using. If you want to use both the onion and cabbage, reduce the total quantity of both vegetables to 2 Tablespoons.

Heat a non-stick Tava with 1 Tablespoon of ghee and spread a ladle of batter into a circular pancake. You can pour a few drops of oil/ghee around the outside of the pancake to help it cook quicker. Keep the heat low to avoid batter sticking to the pan. When done, you can see the sides of the pancake browning and you should be able to slide a Flat pancake-flip underneath it and flip over to the other side. Cook the other side in the same way.

Cook the rest of the pancakes as above. The batter should make between 4-6 pancakes depending on the size. Serve hot with a dollop of butter and a piece of Jaggery. The sweetness of the Jaggery goes very well with the spicy pancake.

Steamed Rice
(Serves 2, takes around 20 minutes)

Ingredients:

Basmati or White Long-grained Rice: 1 Cup

Method:

If you're using a pressure cooker, add 2 ½ Cups of water to the rice and cook until 4-5 whistles. Do not open the cooker for 10-15 minutes as the rice would continue to cook in the steam after you remove it from the heat.

If you are not using a pressure cooker, bring 3-4 Cups of water to boil and add the rice. Cook over low heat for 15-20 minutes. You can check if the rice is done by removing a few grains with a fork and crushing them. If they mash down without resistance, then the rice is cooked.

Lemon Rasam
(Serves 2, takes 40 minutes including cooking the Dal)

Ingredients:

Arhar Dal: ¼ Cup
Green Chilli: 1
Asafoetida: a pinch
Turmeric powder: a pinch
Tomato (Optional): 1
Salt: to taste
Lemon: 1
Coriander leaves: for a garnish
Mustard seeds: 1 Teaspoon
Sesame Oil: 2 Teaspoons

Method:

Cut the Green chilli into small pieces. Cook the Arhar Dal in a pressure cooker or in plenty of boiling water with salt and turmeric powder. In a small saucepan, heat the sesame oil and add the mustard seeds (Tarka). When they splutter, add the Asafoetida and green chillies and stir for 1 minute. Add 2 Cups of warm water, turmeric and the tomato (cut into 2 halves). Bring to a boil and reduce the heat. Drain and mash the cooked Dal and add to the water. Once again, bring the mixture to a boil and remove from heat. Add the juice from the lemon and garnish with Coriander leaves. Check and adjust the salt and serve hot as a delightful soup. You can also mash a few spoonfuls of steamed rice with 2 ladles of Rasam and serve with a dollop of ghee. Rasam-rice is a regular feature on most Tamil menus.

Menu Suggestions

The book has so far given you a combination of dishes that are traditionally cooked on the day. In addition, here are some delightful mix-and-match options using a cross-section of the recipes

Light Snacks/Lunches

MENU 1
- Idlis
- Coconut Chutney
- Sambar

Serve the Idlis with a dollop of chutney and a hot bowl of Sambar to dip in.

MENU 2
- Savoury Urad Modak
- Tomato Raita
- Aubergine Dip

Serve steaming modaks with the chutney/dip combination - delicious!

MENU 3
- Rava Upma
- Tomato Chutney

Dinner menus

Menu 1

• Starter

  - Aloo Bonda

  - Tomato Chutney

• Main Course

  - Tamarind Rice

  - Okra Raita

  - Aubergine Dip

• Dessert

  - Vella Sundal

Serve the main course with Poppadums

Menu 2

• Starter

  - Sundal

• Main Course

  - Paruppu Adai

  - Kalli Kootu

Serve the Adai with a dollop of butter, a piece of jaggery and some warm stew.

• Dessert

  - Chakkara Pongal

MENU 3

• Starter
 - Salt Adai and White Butter

• Main Course
 - Coconut Rice
 - Talakham

• Dessert
 - Poli

MENU 4

• Starter
 - A selection of Diwali Savoury Snacks served with Tomato Chutney

• Main Course
 - Lemon Rasam Rice (see basic recipes)
 - Avial

• Dessert
 - Neyappam

MENU 5

• Starter
- Vadai with Coconut Chutney

• Main Course
- Dosa with Potato or Salsa Filling
- Sambar

• Dessert
- Badam Burfi

index

Indian festive flavours

Salt Adai (Savoury Short pancakes) — 19

Seedai (Fried Savoury Dumpling) — 26

Thattai (Crunchy Rice and Dal Savoury Snack) — 28

Savoury Urad Modak (Steamed Savoury Dumplings) — 30

Sundal (Chickpea Stir-fry) — 34

Aloo Bonda (Potato Croquets) — 40

Rava Upma (Savoury Semolina Porridge) — 42

Tenguyal (Crunchy Cumin Pipes) — 44

Oma Podi (Crispy noodles with Carrom seeds) — 45

Mullu Tenguyal or Chakli (Crunchy Sesame pipes) — 46

Ribbon Pakoda (Spicy Ribbons) — 47

Paruppu Adai (Spicy Lentil Pancakes) — 54

SWEETS AND DESSERTS

Poli (Coconut Pancakes) — 2

Milk Poli (Saffron-milk Pancakes) — 3

Pongal (Rice and Jaggery Pudding) — 6

Sweet Adai (Sweet short pancakes) — 18

Sweet Seedai (Fried Sweet Dumpling) — 27

Sweet Modak (Steamed Coconut Dumplings) — 29

Vella Sundal (Bean Pudding) — 35

Rava Burfi (Semolina Fudge) — 48

Badam Burfi (Almond Fudge) — 49

Ma Ladoo (Dal and Dry Fruit balls) — 50

Vella/Aval Pori (Sweet Puffed/Flaked Rice) — 52

Neyappam (Banana and Jaggery Dumpling) — 53